Is
SOCIAL MEDIA
Helpful or Harmful?

By Jennifer Lombardo

KidHaven
PUBLISHING

Published in 2021 by
KidHaven Publishing, an Imprint of Greenhaven Publishing, LLC
353 3rd Avenue
Suite 255
New York, NY 10010

Designer: Deanna Paternostro
Editor: Jennifer Lombardo

Photo credits: Cover Andrey_Popov/Shutterstock.com; p. 5 Rawpixel.com/Shutterstock.com; p. 7 sitthiphong/Shutterstock.com; p. 9 Dragana Gordic/Shutterstock.com; p. 11 FGC/Shutterstock.com; p. 13 pixinoo/Shutterstock.com; p. 14 malazzama/Shutterstock.com; p. 15 Tinxi/Shutterstock.com; p. 17 (main) Maridav/Shutterstock.com; p. 17 (inset) © iStockphoto.com/milindri; p. 19 (top) © iStockphoto.com/SolStock; p. 19 (bottom) © iStockphoto.com/lesliejmorris; p. 21 (notepad) ESB Professional/Shutterstock.com; p. 21 (markers) Kucher Serhii/Shutterstock.com; p. 21 (photo frame) FARBAI/iStock/Thinkstock; p. 21 (inset, left) MPH Photos/Shutterstock.com; p. 21 (inset, middle-left) Sergey Novikov/Shutterstock.com; p. 21 (inset, middle-right) Twin Design/Shutterstock.com; p. 21 (inset, right) YanLev/Shutterstock.com.

Cataloging-in-Publication Data

Names: Lombardo, Jennifer.
Title: Is social media helpful or harmful? / Jennifer Lombardo.
Description: New York : KidHaven Publishing, 2021. | Series: Points of view | Includes glossary and index.
Identifiers: ISBN 9781534534162 (pbk.) | ISBN 9781534534186 (library bound) | ISBN 9781534534193 (ebook) | ISBN 9781534534179 (set)
Subjects: LCSH: Social media–Juvenile literature. | Online social networks–Juvenile literature. | Internet–Social aspects–Juvenile literature. | Social media–Social aspects–Juvenile literature.
Classification: LCC HM742.L66 2021 | DDC 302.23'1–dc23

Printed in the United States of America

Some of the images in this book illustrate individuals who are models. The depictions do not imply actual situations or events.

CPSIA compliance information: Batch #BS20K: For further information contact Greenhaven Publishing LLC, New York, New York at 1-844-317-7404.

Please visit our website, www.greenhavenpublishing.com. For a free color catalog of all our high-quality books, call toll free 1-844-317-7404 or fax 1-844-317-7405.

Find us on

CONTENTS

Social media is a collection of websites that allow people to interact with each other. It's so common today that almost everyone has at least one account—not just people, but stores, movies, sports teams, and even government **agencies**!

Social media can be a great way to connect with other people, share important things, and learn about what's going on around you. There are a lot of reasons why people believe social media can be helpful. However, there are also many reasons why people believe it can be harmful. Knowing the facts on both sides of this argument is the best way to form your own opinion.

Know the Facts!

As of 2019, the three most popular social media platforms were Facebook, YouTube, and Instagram.

Thanks to smartphones, people can check their social media accounts no matter where they are.

FRIENDS

Most people get a social media account so they can share things with their friends. For example, if someone has a picture they want to show all their friends, it's easier to post it online instead of sending it to everyone they know. People also use social media to learn other people's opinions. For example, someone who's thinking about taking a vacation might make a post asking people where they should go.

Some people think social media is a good way to share things with friends and learn about other people, but not everyone feels this way. Some people think social media takes up too much of our time and can be bad for us.

Know the Facts!

Experts say the average person spends almost two and a half hours each day on social media and messaging apps.

Social media lets people share their thoughts and feelings right away.

ENOUGH

Some people don't think "liking" posts on social media is a way to be a good friend. They worry that people who use social media a lot aren't making authentic, or real, connections to other people because they're not paying attention to others in person. Instead, they're spending their time on their smartphones or computers.

It's been said that social media makes us lonelier. When people spend a lot of time online, they might not see people as often in person. This can make them feel **isolated**. Many people say spending less time on social media can help fix this.

Know the Facts!

Handwritten letters are often seen as more personal and authentic than social media posts. When two people become friends by writing to each other, they're called "pen pals." Many pen pals like to send handwritten letters, even today.

Sometimes people use social media to **cyberbully** others. It's often easier for people to say mean things online than it is in person.

WORLD

Social media has made it easier for people to learn about different **cultures**. On some platforms, such as YouTube, people can make public posts that teach others what life is like in another country. This makes it easier to understand that people who might seem very different from you actually have more in common with you than you think!

People can use social media to stay in touch with friends who have moved away. Social media also allows people to make friends who live in other places. This helps people feel less lonely. Sending letters to people who live in other places can be fun, but it takes a long time to get them. It's much faster to talk on social media.

Know the Facts!

Studies show that 57 percent of teens have made friends online with someone they'd never met in person before.

Social media has connected people around the world. This helps us learn about other ways of life and become more understanding and accepting of all kinds of people.

Is It SAFE?

Many people worry that social media isn't safe, especially for kids. They think it doesn't give people enough privacy and it can connect them with people who are dangerous, or not safe to talk to or meet. Social media users need to always be careful about what they share online and who they share it with.

Sometimes a person pretends to be a different person online. This has caused some people to worry about being harmed by a person who's pretending to be someone else. If someone online asks you things that make you uncomfortable, don't answer them! Log off, and tell an adult.

Know the Facts!

Most social media platforms have age restrictions. Kids under 13 can't sign up. Some kids pretend to be older, even though that's breaking the rules.

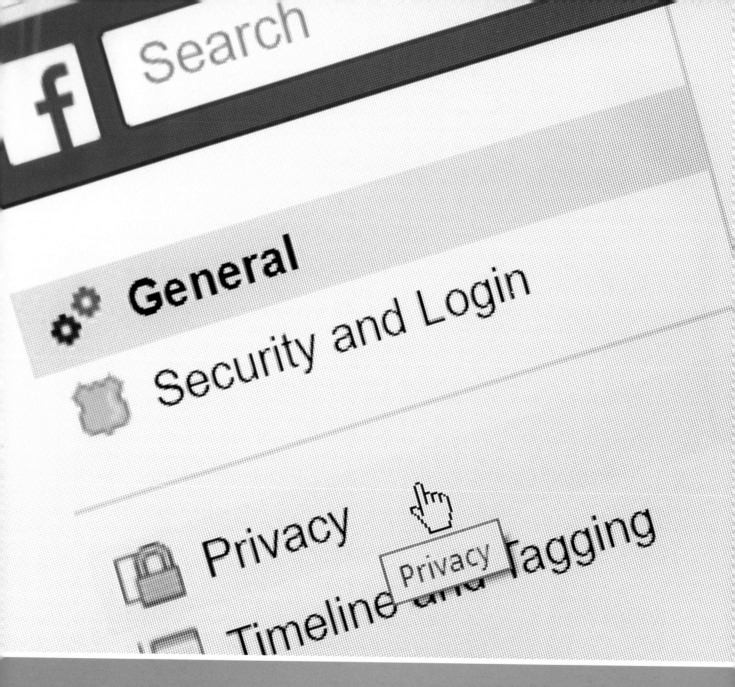

f Search

General

Security and Login

Privacy

Timeline and Privacy Tagging

People can set their social media accounts to "private" to control who sees what they post. However, many people worry about the websites themselves getting people's private **information**.

Getting Out
THERE

Often, connections on social media go past the computer and into the "real world." Some people think of social media users as isolated people sitting alone for hours in front of their computer, but this isn't true for most people.

One way people can use social media to be more social in person is by making a post about their plans so their friends can decide whether they want to join in. Another way is by checking different **organizations'** social media pages to learn about events they can go to in their community.

Meetup

Know the Facts!

An app called Meetup lets people join groups, take part in activities in their community, and make new friends who share a common interest.

Organizations often post on social media platforms about events they're hosting, such as a painting class.

LIFE

When people post things on social media, they're often picking the best parts of their life to show others. This can give people who see these posts the idea that their life isn't as good as other people's, which is why too much time spent on social media can make them feel sad.

It's important to remember that social media doesn't always show the real story. For example, a girl might post a photo of her and her friends laughing together. Someone who sees it might say, "I wish I had a good friendship like that." However, the friends might have had a fight right after taking the photo.

Know the Facts!

Sometimes people share fake news stories on social media. These are false stories made to look like real news. Remember that not everything you read is true!

Some people post fake vacation photos by standing in front of a poster or by changing the photo to make it look like it was taken somewhere else. It's important to remember that not everything you see online is real.

OTHERS

Social media can be used to raise awareness and give people ways to help after something bad happens in the world, such as a hurricane. People can also use social media to let their friends and family know they're safe if they live where a scary event took place.

Some social media platforms have started making it easier for people to **donate** money to organizations that are important to them. For example, Facebook lets people make fundraising pages and share them with friends and family. Many people have begun doing this for their birthday instead of asking for presents for themselves.

Know the Facts!

In 2019, when Hurricane Dorian hit the Bahamas, Facebook offered to match its users' donations to the Red Cross.

Some people use social media to ask friends and family to donate money to an organization they support, such as an organization that helps animals or one that helps elderly people.

Forming an
OPINION

Most people agree that social media isn't all good or all bad. It's how someone uses it that makes it one or the other. For example, using social media for a few minutes a day might help someone keep in touch with their friends, but using it for several hours can make them feel isolated. Checking social media instead of doing homework or getting enough sleep can also be harmful to people.

Some people think social media is more helpful than harmful. Other people think the opposite. Now that you know both sides of the argument, what do you think?

Know the Facts!

As of 2019, 3.2 billion people use social media. That's almost half the people in the world!

Is social media helpful or harmful?

HELPFUL

- It helps people stay in touch with their friends and form new friendships.

- It helps people understand different cultures.

- It lets people know about events they can go to.

- It's used to raise awareness and money for good causes.

HARMFUL

- It can cause people to spend less time forming authentic friendships in person.

- People can be bullied through social media.

- It isn't always safe.

- It can make people feel bad about themselves by comparing their life to others'.

Whether you think social media is helpful or harmful, you should remember to take time away from it to enjoy other activities.

GLOSSARY

agency: A government department that is responsible for a certain activity or area.

app: Short for application; a computer program made to run on a cell phone or tablet.

culture: The beliefs and ways of life of a certain group of people.

cyberbully: To bully someone through online or cell phone messages or posts.

donate: To give something in order to help a person or organization.

expert: Someone who has a special skill or knowledge.

information: Knowledge or facts about something.

isolated: Separated from others.

organization: A group formed for a specific purpose.

restriction: A limit or control on something.

For More
INFORMATION

WEBSITES

KidsHealth: "Online Safety"
kidshealth.org/en/kids/online-id.html
Learn more about staying safe online.

Media Smarts: Educational Games
mediasmarts.ca/digital-media-literacy/educational-games
This website features many interactive games that teach children about privacy, bias, cyberbullying, and digital literacy.

BOOKS

Gregory, Josh. *Posting on Social Media*. New York, NY: Children's Press, 2019.

Larson, Paul J. *Social Media*. Huntington Beach, CA: Teacher Created Materials, 2017.

Woolf, Alex. *Let's Think About the Internet and Social Media*. Chicago, IL: Heinemann Library, 2015.

INDEX